Autodidactic

Autodidactic

DON KERR

Brick Books

CANADIAN CATALOGUING IN PUBLICATION DATA

Kerr, Don
Autodidactic

Poems.
ISBN 0-919626-92-0

I. Title.

PS8571.E71A97 1997   C811'.54   C97-931181-0
PR9199.3.E33A97 1997

We acknowledge the support of the Canada Council for the Arts
for our publishing programme, and the support of the University of
Saskatchewan for this book. The support of the Ontario Arts
Council is also gratefully acknowledged.

Some of these poems have appeared in *Arc, Quarry,
The New Quarterly,* and *Matrix.*

The cover image, 'Poplar Breeze' (1986), is an acrylic stain
by Robert Sinclair.

The typeface is Galliard,
and the stock is acid-free Zephyr Antique laid.
Printed and bound by The Porcupine's Quill Inc.

Brick Books
431 Boler Road, Box 20081
London, Ontario, N6K 4G6

I 2 3 4 • 99 98 97

to good drivers
        mildred & david
to good hosts
        bernadette & wilf

I.

my father waited for the train to pass
his arm resting in the sun   the hot winds of July
travelling hundreds of miles
the train slowly gathering speed
he shut off the motor   the prairie
rushed in   whispering
under the train's roar   counting cars
and forgot at twenty four   eyes looking
so far   how far   freight train   freight train
goin west   lumber and grain
he took out his BA notebook
remembering to write in the last
oil change   the train
whistling the next grid
gathering speed   the century
a third over   hand on the gear shift
the sweet prairie rushing in
my father waiting

lets out the clutch

gathering speed
in a wake of spun gravel

2.

my father read the paper
as if the news were important
he jotted his mileage in notebooks
he could keep in a shirt pocket
When my friend Ed got older
he kept seeing in his own face
the face of his father
and as the days went one way
memory went another
the Philadelphia of his youth
the exciting turn-of-the-century
babble of new life on Hester Street
this side of the water
In the photograph my father and his friends
have just finished playing tennis
and smile through the camera
at the audience they never imagined
What will they do next?
drop the limburger down the heat vent
into the girls' apartment in the Riviera
form the anti-oscillation league
chop up the school walk in Gull Lake
for heat on their way to the World's Fair
in Chicago

finding their way here
by devious routes

3.

I looked at his face and I swore
I would make up for lost time
I swore I would make up
for lost time
his face like a radio stars
I looked for a long time
waiting for that train to pass
engraving that face
saying this is where I begin
this is where my new life
begins.

4.

the world in which we sit has such substance
the orchard   the garden   the houses
such a benign sky in Kamloops
the water sprinklers in the apple trees
whispering   whisper
the day away
that faint motor driving off
the day we sit beneath
drawing on the day   thin as air
the old streets in their squares
regular as sprinklers on the bright grass
in the evening walking home
at the bottom of the neighborhood
ribbed by elms   the streets whispering
secrets of water

5.

our voices after breakfast
in the pause before travelling
the sun promising we'll be real
all day long   chevrolet
carving the hills   the mountains
the valleys thickening into oases
losing all their literal trees
and sparkling   literally sparkling
like the valley of our dreams

6.

he pencilled sums in the margins of newspapers
in notebooks and scribblers   adding it up
did the old-fashioned long division
sitting at the north end of the
enamel kitchen table
his pencils in a cup
on the corner bracket
his faithful car waiting
the numbers adding up
the job for thirty years
the house growing smaller
as the family grew larger
now when we open doors
the ghosts scurry
into the edges of the house
no vacuum can find
nosing under beds
no scouring or quick turns
in the attic   the coal bin
the shelves   under the stairs
on the back stoop we leave
a glass of beer a plate
of bacon and eggs
in the morning
the lawn has been mown
the garden weeded
we hear a car in the alley
run to the back gate   it's just
turned the corner
you can hear the wheels
muttering on the gravel

7.

there was in our family no story told
of babies by surprise or lovers wild
as the night wore on
of suicides or fortunes made
ours was a world of family picnics
at Deep Cove   the day gorgeous
my favorite cousin and her boyfriend
the son of coca cola and I
in the pines up the hill
the blue cove saying this
is where blue comes from
making fun of the family
the aunts and the uncles
spreading food on the picnic tables
and we the family rebels
going as far as we would ever go
with an unkind word

our rite of passage
into helping out for life

we re-entered of our own accord

8.

the boy had three friends
when he was young
Stoggie Stugit and Grunkle
who were smarter than anybody
whose mothers could cook better than yours
who no one ever met but him
and they played in his mind
all the years of his life
His family is in the room
his wife is talking to him
a party rages
he is looking right at you
and is already elsewhere
walking with his fantastic friends
who he calls for the moment
past road and want
The present's a prison
however at times green
and he's always
walking out
faithless
every day of his life
loving
the highway the car
driving
rapidly away
out of the present

9.

Tom said he didn't know why
they had fences on cemeteries
Nobody can get out
and nobody wants in
In a rain of sun the young man was buried
The town is in the graveyard now
Transport trucks booming like thunder
down the highway
We walk back to the Kuroki town hall
for sandwiches cake and coffee
Tom aged eighty says c'mon
and we step into the dark beer parlour
Tom unhinges his throat
and pours them in
It's okay they won't catch us
if we're fast enough

10.

maybe twelve of us on bikes
and Billy from three doors down
a skinny two storey without a porch
forgot to watch his little sister
who ran out between the bikes
and was hit by a car was
run over and the driver weeping
I never saw her I never saw her
she just ran out and Billy running
home and the rest of us thinking well
it wasn't my fault it wasn't
my fault
not looking at the broken girl
like a dead cat

II.

of stories we remember
the parts the telling has kept
David was doing a finger painting
and I asked well what is it?
I don't know I'm not finished yet.

and when he was finished,
well then what is it?
I don't know.
I've never seen one of those before.

there was a third question
and a third answer I can't remember.
It was the house on Elliott
under the great elms
but the look of the boy
the day or what came next
or before   my head
full as a house
gone

12.

how can there be,
this long blue lake
deep with promise
the small white sails
tacking into the wind
shoving them over the water
their waves larger
than the wind's waves
how can there be,
this sky so blue,
    dark secrets
    anger
    revenge

nature is never
guilty of guilt

no cloud in the sky
however unfaithful
was ever baptised

man can imagine
he fell from a garden
he digs and disinters

the last word in evolution
wave on
lake wave on

the cars go by
as quickly as a wink

slicing the wind
like butter

13.

there is no sound to sunlight
but the rushing through it
a waterfall pounding in the ear
over and over   the window of the car
open   the arm a hostage to sunlight
this is the sound of going places
past the last spike
and the three valley gap
and the yards with willows
whose hair has never been cut
the sound I want is the sound
the sun makes on my page
at 70 miles an hour

now

lemme tell you about my neighborhood
and an unknown but important fact
acourse in those days there were
bread wagons and milk wagons
run by horse power and ice wagons
we stole chunks a ice rubbin off the straw
in the back alley where there was can-the-can
or back alley cricket until we allowed the
bunt and hit that ruined the game
tried fox and hounds good guys and Germans
the neighbourhood growing up
houses and trees but alla that stuff well
that happens everywhere but you see
what was really special about our neighbourhood
is that God grew up there
that's it   God grew up there
playin hide and seek
goin to school
Roman Catholic acourse
good at homework bad at athletics
two grade eight girls had a crush on him
but he was workin on his sums and tenses
he wasn't interested in harps
or the hit parade
but he sure liked baseball
like the diamond and the rules
and if you made a good play or not
it was perfectly clear and a lot bettern
hockey he kept the score card
he came second in class
to a girl who became a nun
but he was a really angelic alterboy
and had a terrific memory
when I meet him on Broadway
for a coffee he can remember every detail
about those days like he was still there

15.

the camera jiggled
so the photo's spoilt
a slight haze   a slight daze
over everything in sight
as if no one stood still

this photo's a success
they stand stock still
staring out
farther than the eye can see
across entire decades
saying every time
father son brother lover
you're a dead man

16.

I never in city
had the least use for country
neither haybarn nor harvesting
saddles or sloughs
pored over maps and photos
from the high gloss
National Geographic
and knew by heart
Yosemite and Takkakaw Falls
Going to the Sun and the Snake River
Canyon the high green mountains
and the white streams finding their way
over rocks and fallen trees
the clicks of the View Master
the promise of a cool corner
in a large room furnished
like no other in town or country
let me sit by mountain streams
cause I'm just a prairie boy

17.

at daydown the mountains
folding in on themselves
the cloud on the far left
is up for a citation
in category 2b   beautiful cloud
of the cream-coloured variety
entered by Merle Littlejohn
of Spilmacheen and took second prize
in the World Cloud Competition
the residents of Barstow
unincorporated are so proud
they display it weekly
over the headwaters
of the Columbia Valley

18.

now we travel in the half light
that warms the world
the forest consists
of many individual trees
each of which is now in the sun
perfectly clear and distinct
a green inclining to yellow
and at the door of the valley the dazzling
is beyond words
    the alchemy of evening
    the gilding of the sky
    the memory tree branching out
    the thick bulrush and the open-mouthed lily
    meet in the same slough
    the Purcells a blue wave
    about to break in dreams
    all through the night
87 miles to journey's end
fooled again we want again
the suspense to last

19.

journey's end is now assured
turn right at the gas station
with the motel attached
sharp right past the Terra Vista
condominiums then the T turn
past Shangri La and there
at lake front
journey's end
no better can be imagined
a lake of rye whiskey
the Purcells straight up
the skies full of fat clouds
like comforters
in the cabin there is always bridge
over troubled times

20.

all the stars in the sky
have come out tonight
the still ones   the fallen ones
and across the lake the railroad star
at a snail's pace creeping
its load of coal and whistling
in the dark on its way to golden
sheet lightning over the purcells

the stars are so many heroes
escorted by poets into heaven
orion and cassandra and john a
macdonald and tommy douglas

train whistles invermere down the track
the silent stars upon their invisible track
and one like the train moving steady
and slow through the high heavens
the astrologer
throws up his hands the poet grows
ashamed of his inordinate love
of machines upon
a single track

or was it written in the stars
regular as wheels and boxcars
from the beginning

21.

the lake that enters the eye
enters the heart   enters the
intricate delta land of the nervous system
on this morning
                    a breath of wind
on the still water
the motor of the body
                    turning over
step by step the slow going out
to meet the water
                    and slipping under
trying not to enter but become
                            the other
soft strokes disturb the water least
and best is the immersion of the dead man's float
see level   eye level   the world
                    turns here

22.

on the road to the dump
rattling over washboard
the mountains impassive
the golf course in green
the regional refuse disposal
    lunchroom for bears
    paradise for bulldozers
    everyone's closet
    everyone's subconscious
    everyone's dump
the sign that we're hard at work
keeping the economy on the move
like a car on the road
or a house going up
the embryonic balcony overlooking
lake and sun
turn on the transistor
that turns on the carpenter
who turns the screw
that builds the house
that turns the tap
that fills the dump
that jack made

23.

at the White House Hotel
John Wayne in the sky
over the wagon train
is the setting sun
on the west wall
signed best wishes
a carved bear carries a fish in its paw
there's the Kokanee twist cap
you wear on your head
twist to remove or
hold it steady
and someone twists your head
I don't want a beer I want
a minute
at the White House Hotel in Windermere
the radio nagging
the eggs pickling
the waitress polishing off
mountain sketches   us polishing off
draft beer at eleven in the morning
our short sleeves waiting for the sun
that makes the day in Yemen
where the talker works the rigs the sun
is to survive   but here
under the awning of a hat in vacationland
sun is to take   and take   and take it
easy   the ghost of John Wayne
smiling down upon us from
over the fireplace
the day stretching down the lake
like we're gonna do
let's move out
yo

24.

on the roof of the world
clouds gather
an osprey hovers
plunges into the wrinkling lake
in its talons a trout
thrashing its wings for height

under the roof of the world
the three hundred thousand dollar
summer homes climb the bare hills
dreaming of lakeshore
dreaming of city
as at home in this world
as the barbed wire fence
the regional refuse dump

on the roof of the world
the osprey hovers
hunching its shoulders
in the great plunge
the lake at evening
like glass the clouds
climbing out of the purcells
the car can kill
whatever it takes us to

25.

at the decanting of the will
how shall the lake be divided
and the goods gathered over a lifetime
to which grandchild the belleek
the dinner setting   the silver
the sofa   the bedstead   the tools
the house that will not sell
(the town so out of demand)
the half bottle of rye
the green graves
the cabin shall go
to whoever is good for it
and of the lake the water
to each according to his strokes
I want to bid on the following items
the portulaca   the butterfly hinges
in the old house   swallows in the eavestroughs
the drive to the lake down hallways of trees
the bloody farmers haven't harvested yet
for handouts
the lakefront property has just been bought
the cabin has yet to be moved   trees cleared
the first pier point its finger
into the lake   which is already there
the evergreens yet to be planted
the plywood rabbit yet to be cut
the stones to be gathered and painted
there is as yet no ignorant neighbour
with a yard light to ward off
dangerous stars

just before it all happens
is of this estate
the share
I claim

26.

so many friends
fallen into the abyss
there for a summer
in the shadow of the pulled drapes
ice cubes by the cold air vents
the nina simone summer?
the oscar brown summer?
they walked out under the trees
one by one
and fell into the abyss
until there is no one to talk to
about those summers
the pimms summer
the gin and tonic summer
fallen like so many friends
without a word fallen
into the abyss we imagine
as just round the corner
to swallow so many
vanishing friends

27.

the holy time is quiet
as the kids the nuns
told to be quiet
the water the wind controls
in its rows of waves
says next to nothing
the sky awash with blue robes
white wimples   this lake
settling under the absolute night
whispering to shore
its every tactile delight

28.

it all comes out in the wash

this is the part that covers the part
of you

the lascivious line and the lure
of the wash

primary passions primary colours
blowin in the wind and there is no
other member of today's audience
responding as I do to the thinnest
narrowest parts of your
second skin

or what's an imagination for

29.

tuning the marriage
   one string at a time
you play keyboard
   and I'll play rhyme
your fingers moving down waves
   on this long lake
playing the rib cage
   in the gathering dark
high notes promise delicate care
   the whole night through
bass notes promise darkening scare
   the whole night through
the balancing of pleasure
   the whole night through

30.

the light gathering
   all in one corner
the dreams gathering
   just out of sight
the child holding
   her mind to herself
says tell me a story
   the one she knows
over and over and after
   how far does she go
            on the night waves

and you singing
   the old familiar songs
the light gathering
   all in one corner
the song gone travelling
   on the night waves
and you before us are
   awash with journey
   bourne from which no
   starlit waters
   over the edge where you
   are the stranger

and on this night return to us
you are yourself or the other
drop anchor here or there
bobbing up and down
the dangerous
            the dark the
      scary the
   sweet
night

31.

the songs call back
the long departed souls
this was her favorite
          five foot two
his favorite
          darktown strutters
my buddy no buddy
just like you
fetched from the dark
by the dancing fiddle
the two-handed piano
the long departed gather
          in the darkening room
at daybreak we drive
out of the mountains
and across the prairie
playing the dead out of every
yellow-grass cemetery
on highways eight and five
we do it for politic's sweet self
(the N D P needs every rural vote it can get
dead or alive)

32.

Dumont rides a bronze horse
by the river where once
or so it was told
he rode a buffalo
down the prairie
that grew the downtown
he shot it   climbed it
knife in hand and it
reared up and rode off
or so it was told
Dumont upon its shaggy back
who has for children of all ages
fifty bullets left for the soldiers
invading the prairie like hail
like rust   like drought
over-running the underdogs
in the shallow rifle pits
shooting nails and dying
Dumont sliding down the river bank
clutching at saskatoons and riding
fifty bullets down the river
reined in on Spadina
riding through the mown grass
of the winners

33.

each valley you travel
is the beginning of memory
there are before you
the literal the stalwart trees
and the kootenay rushing its green way
upstream against traffic
there are passing lanes and mountain passes
in the high clouds and they are all
invisible as air
and travel
every hour of the day for
the fifth occupant of the car
is memory

34.

there are amongst us
the fanatics of news
every hour on the hour
fearful lest history
pass them by
the crisis in the middle east
occur without their participation
the fanatics of news
know the sweetness of the days
they travel through
is false   live upon
war and its alarums
in faraway places with strange sounding names
and of this highway know great joy
for it carves in halves the earth
it lashes down with this long rope
and the fanatics of news upon
its very top drive at 70
75 80 burning with joy
the irreplaceable gas and steaming
up the sky   no longer just a
watcher but a maker
of crisis   and alive
in their own time
burning up the highway
drawing down armageddon
the fanatics of news anticipating
eagerly hour by hour
the final ambush round any corner

35.

coming out of the mountains
onto the prairie
the body settling
the eyes opening
the clouds swelling
the heart filling
the mind thinking again
upon the last things always
   the turn for home
   the state of the vegetable garden
   the state of the flower garden
   whether the abandoned dog will return
   our affection
   the streets remain in the order
   in which they were placed

36.

stopping between highways
hush puppies still doing
20 miles an hour
open-faced sandwich
cream of cauliflower soup
and hi-balling Calgary
the downtown towers
in the distance like a tray
of hi-balls anyway
this rapid chevrolet
driving the commercial excresents
the stop and go   the diesel fumes
let us now compare famous
franchises

all those years ago
the clouds from the mountains
sheltered this boy practicing his putting
into a soup can buried in the back lawn
never so well so often mowed
and on the golf course
having read the golf books
and swung by theory
he sliced three straight
on the fourteenth
into a farmer's field
before a lovely chip shot
skidded over the sand green
and he one-putted for a nine
Golf being a game of the immediate future
while walking through the saskatoons to the fifteenth
he looked right past the last hole and thought
maybe he should give up golf   being a lefty
and fated to slice and preferring
the book and the theory   become a poet
or at least an intellectual

38.

for years after it was over
I'd still wait in the beer parlor
for my friends to drop in
knowing they'd spun off
to other cities
other lives
drinking the first round
with the ghosts of good times past
that first warm smell of the draft
the long day waiting in the heat
for its corners to be invented
the city laid out solely to serve
the drinking classes   the sun to bake us
to make us thirst   the girls to baste
our tender egos   if girls
were our taste   the chinese cafes
to fill our empty spaces
spun one by one across the country
like every party ended one by one
till only the three of us left
opened the six pack   they now dead
by the hand of liquor
and all that drove them
into its lovely arms
the love of jesus and the love of men
on the outs with hearth
and home   they had
such good taste

that man knew Berryman
and this man Yeats
would you be willing to be interviewed?
they say and I say wait
till we've met someone
everyone knows is first rate
and they say who?
well in Montreal there's
someone met Cohen
and the coast thinks the gulf stream's
the main stream but the great plain
is next door to the great plain
and our metropolitan areas
are secondary and tertiary at best
it is the role of the margin
to be marginalized
the role of the hinterland
to hint
     in lower case
     our only caps
are baseball caps
farm machinery caps
or twist off caps

this woman knew Lowell
and that woman Larkin
now I got a list but I'm loyal
I'm taciturn
a plain man
it's the role of the uncanonized
not to provoke the gods
to be the anon of canon
let others be the small bore

but for goodness sake
what of w & r & b & k
well I'd say
it's too early to tell

40.

when you travel together
you meet each other
coming and going
talking your way back
in a car leaning
into the next bend
weathering the same
road construction the same
95 above at kalispell
road thick with cars   chasing
the same bed for the night the same
going to the sun heritage
highway you fall off
you starve to death
before hitting bottom the same
motel in wenatchee choosing
steak and tequila
and corn like eating
old gold
on the road again
all day long
at close quarters
liking it still

41.

there are tonight on the prairies
a sky for each corner of the sky
   a rain forest
   ramparts of grandeur
   a pale blue lake
   rear projection of sundown
not a mountain in sight
nor a body of water
only acreages   parkland
come visit the miniature trees
of the prairies
the highway now dreaming us
into the wide mouth
of the sky

42.

I am the desperado in love
I married a woman
I had children
I live in a house
It has a family den
I come home for supper
I park in the driveway
I hold down a steady job
I am the desperado in love
weedin and washin
wipin and wivin

43.

modern is
white and cubed
and has windows wrapped
round the corners of houses
modern jumps around
like remote control
I have enjoyed a very modern summer
bust in bits and pieces and
adding up to something or other
modern has no vibrato
modern has no inhibitions
about replacing the world
no illusions
modern doesn't serve fried eggs
for breakfast
modern suspects of grandparents
their long continuity
except for the couple who divorced at 90
after the children had all died

44.

we learn to accept small mercies
the Benolkin Block of 1909
built by a grandfather of an uncle
visited as a kid in those coal burning days
learned in the small dark livingroom
high low jack and game
is now a much affronted
set of professional offices
cedar papering over brick but it is
hanging on and low down
one maple left in the back yard
next door to set it off
the Milroy Apartments
22 storeys and not one of them
worth reading
a building without character
mood thought or theme
a printout building
and no passage of time
will promote it and yet
its very presence
density at all costs and levels promotes
the Benolkin Block
circa 1909
a small mercy

45.

in the car on its wheels
you can still feel
the feel of the road
the rough pavement
the oiled strips
where the frost breaks
the pen skittering over the page
gathering speed out of Hanna
it's our world we drive
the reassuring fences
the turns where the turns
always were   every thirty miles
freight train approaching
its diamond jubilee on the
goose lake line
the sky smooth as a lake
or power steering
or a good journey
felt all the way down
all the way through

46.

we have each our own waterfall
our bridal veil our bow our cascade
our valley our lake our idea
of idyllic and it feeds us
at breakfast in the cafe
people at every table
the food fried   the coffee
a black stream in the guts
the constitutional
when the need arises
we can always work ourselves up
to our valley   our stream
the water falling in curves
cool in the sun

Hot Spot

that woman'll be the death of me

walkin in the heat
with less and less on
a bit of breeze off the lake
and a sunhat
in the bush leagues
the hot spot

hot spot

hottern hell out
new delhi   djakarta   miami
eat your heart out
we're the hot spot
athens   bahamas   you name it
we're the hot spot we're prairie
fire on highway five
tell the gas jockey in roblin
hottest spot in the world's right here
she says no wonder I'm so damn hot
I ain't goin back out there

that woman'll be the death of me

cookin along
apron that says
I'm a real dish
moves when she does
it's gettin real hot in

pay attention world
we're the hot spot
sun's set his eye
on the western plains
so hey pay attention
goin for a hundred
in the shade
not a cloud in the sky
but nobody's lookin
not a car on the road
or a newsman in sight
no first resort or famous spa
off the course and in the rough
we're where nobody drops in
for a look and that really
pisses me off

pay attention world
we're the hot spot

that woman'll be the death of me

    the pot boiling over
    the taste that makes you want to taste
    taste
    the colossal thirst of a hangover's
    hangover
    he's very well hungover
    she said

had lunch at the hot spot

at moon lake the water
teaches the sky
how to be blue
wish I had a camera
the cyma recta curve of the woman
in the pink hot pants lying on her side
in the shade and the big bum of the lake
shoved into the stuck-up hill
conifer hill
moon lake mooning
pink hip displacing air
eureka rosehip stirs
me up lake wiggles
into shore
hot spot
yeh

that woman'll be the death of me

    nurse me in my final decline
    spent like a wave
    or an old dime
    or a bottlecap stepped into an alley
    or a playground walked on by kids

woman'll be the death of me

    the redemption stanza
    thank you for the privilege
    of letting me share my death
    with you

hot time in the old quarter section
or don't look back

we're on the other side of the lake
but don't look back
you'll get a crick in the neck
record breaking sun in both official temperatures
any crick'll do I say   they say
don't look back

we drive the road before us
or what's a straight road for
ride right over the next minute and
don't look back

slice the land in half
picked clean of cover
burnt trees in piles
evidence everywhere
of the famous Saskatchewan land barrens

they don't look back
ploughdown a straight line
or what's a combine for
gnaw down parkland
or what's a parkland for
big teeth beavers on government grants

who put the chew in Saskatchewan
who took the far outa **far**mer

the great levellers
from parkland to prairie to desert
and we're all in the greenhouse now

the CO_2 the cars exhale
the trees devour   the heat settles under
sun chews wheat gum and
the teeth of the trees are yanked

hot time in the old quarter section
ploughdown tonight

once a beaver's chewed down
every tree in sight
his only hope's a zoo
here on yr right's the family farmer
he's the one with the buzz saw
throw him a tree he's a great cut up
once common on the western plains
throw him a subsidy
he can still mate and all that
but he et his own habitat

and don't look back
you might see where you come from

(o the farmer is the man)

   that woman that woman'll be
   the death of me

      rootin in a flower bed
      tequila sittin in the pantry
      wind can't keep her hands off
      sun climbs outa bed for another hot day in the
      sun
      rootin in a flower bed
      she's a real pro
      file a real
      handful

heat's just a word

the heat's on
hot spot in the old town
tonight the argument
heated up heat me daddy
got me a heater so what's
heat all about
slow burn
back burner
heat's on

we've crossed the border
into critics' country
shut the door helen
let's talk about it

and honey there's no way out
the enigma machine
the opaque cartel
the code of the west
plant yr own thicket
never saw one of those before
word us girls
ah the blessed oblique
salvation for page hogs
and line drivers
text appeal
a thousand words
and still circling

we talked through that night
I never laid a hand on you
enough to make it matter
however thickly ferociously sweetly
desire pounded we
opened our mouths and

       talked

so what else is new
there's only one place for a tongue
god grant a return to realism
we can talk about it after
(in the old way)

  woman'll be woman'll be

    music to my ears
    sun's blowin trumpet
    and the moon's aswarm
    with the heebie jeebies
    sun blows her all over town
    little white fidgety fingers
    in all the old
    familiar places

every sky has a silver cloud

at portage la prairie a cloud appeared from outa nowhere
a silver dollar from an empty hand
we burdened it with all our hopes
for shade

      rain

         bumper
crops   wealth   high salaries   bread basket
of the world   road
            to the new jerusalem
grid road to heaven
gravelled with good hope

o cloud   o cloud   o claude
           lorraine
rain
     purveyer of vistas
     cool dawn trembling
     into evening sleep so certain
     in so certain a world
     cool with distance

by winnipeg the one had multiplied
into the many   a scout pack of clouds
and by mid afternoon they'd all
vanished   evaporated   eaten alive
by the cannibal sun

        or

how to lose weight on the prairies

sit in the sun and let it burn off
skin after skin till yr down to yr
cool night skeleton the

                            winds

blow through

I married a screen door
a hundred small openings on a

                                   hot

       night

um   um   um   um
                    and so on   umm

um   um

ummmm

that woman'll be the heat of me

    I'm dyin ta
    river's sluggish soakin
    in heat   overhung
    parched   dyin ta
    take the plunge

got the hots

turgid river thick with overhang
too tired to move   too hot
to move   ill fed by sun
steaming its brown ancient entrails
assiniboine lowering house values
dog days in the high temperature district
world leaders in bloody-minded sun
but who's looking
brown as last year's autumn styles
dry as a case of empties
two trees fighting over the same dog
hot as steaming as compulsive as
my want for you spreading like sun
over top of me hot coffee hotting
from the inside out all in a sweat about
het up about fret about bet about
whether you really will be the cuppa
hot summer I'm drowning in splashing
in lay my poem book on the grass
see what it'll pick up a twig or two
dry grass root nothing that's got a patch
on you picking me

  o woman'll be the death of me
  o woman'll

    get up a heada steam
    whistlin like a teapot
    I'm a little something
    pour me out sweethot it's
    teatime she hooks
    her little finger I'm a goner
    goin down for the third time

low down sun
unzipperin winnipeggers
up and down the aubrey road
in and out the aberdeen
where we all hang out
aura lee aura lee
you are the one
you make me happy
before the book's begun
makin book on who'll
outshout the sun

woman'll be the death of me
light of my death of me

sun turns a blind eye
on the woman I love
turn the other cheek hon
outflank the shafta
time and the timeless
brown yr beauty spot
honey   hot spot
right here
hotta
haveta
hey

morning in Winnipeg

heat's in training
doin its warmups

I'm walkin
large lady watering
her new turf
two minutes for hip checking

stone bird on a dry bird bath
art

the old on Wolsely
the young in one another's
in trays

black-waisted dishy
young mother

tree or two
undistinguished morning
body on underdrive
only the pen's erect
faint echoes of desire

the lady vanishes

today it's all over   heat wave seat wave
and there are clouds
and the clouds are
                    touching

indiscriminately all over winnipeg

there is a

            breeze

and the body has vanished
no telling how I walk now

time picked up speed why it's so
fast I can't even see it move anymore

women walk by by the score
or so I'm told but I'm cool
I'm a screen door

stanza on home remedies

   do my delicates on cycle four
   dish it out and lay it on the
   hang it on the line
   you made yr bed you gotta
   take it off the back burner

   and the moral of the story is
   snatch victory

woman'll be

autodidactic

I learned on the job.
I learned how not to drive
outrun by a horse on my maiden voyage.
I learned how to do the 180
in case there was a cow on the prairie
or some other interesting phenomenon.
I learned the one-arm tan.
I learned boys sit behind fathers
girls behind mothers.
I learned road maps.
I learned jazz is the driving music.
I learned space and time are mixed
like the smoke from two cigarettes.
I learned navigation.
I learned to be an itinerant writer.
My muse is Hermes god of Exxon.
I learned on the job.
I learned how to be driven around
every long bend from California
to the Kootenay Valley.
I began to learn before memory began.
I learned the taste of gravel
in Saskatchewan country
and the taste of fear
on the hairpins to Takkakaw.
I learned the pleasure of speed
of conquering towns
unzipping the world
what it was like
to live again in my own century
on the road again.

TERRY STEFFEN

Don Kerr is a poet, editor, playwright, and teacher living in Saskatoon. His four previous books of poetry have been widely praised. His publications include history and short stories, and his dramatic works have been performed onstage and on CBC radio. He served as an editor of *Grain* for many years, and has edited anthologies of plays, poems, and political essays.